EXTR
BASKETBALL
STORIES
FOR YOUNG
ATHLETES

13-17

ALL-STAR READS

THIS BOOK BELONGS TO:

....

....

....

....

....

— EXTREME —
BASKETBALL
STORIES
FOR YOUNG
ATHLETES

13-17

ALL-STAR READS

Extreme Basketball Stories for Young Athletes

Copyright © 2023 by All-Star Reads

TABLE OF CONTENTS

INTRODUCTION 9

The Miracle on Ice Court 15

The Shot Heard Around the World 21

The Double-Nickel Game 27

The Lob City Era 33

The Dream Team 39

The Flu Game 45

The Malice at the Palace 51

The Unstoppable Streak 57

The Dunk of Defiance 63

The King's Coronation 69

The Perfect Season 75

The Eurostep Maestro 81

The Shot Clock Savior 87

The Cinderella Story 93

The Upset of the Century 99

CONCLUSION 105

ABOUT US 114

INTRODUCTION

"Basketball is more than a game; it's a platform for dreams to become reality and for ordinary people to achieve extraordinary feats. The stories of the men who have graced this sport are a testament to the power of dedication, resilience, and the relentless pursuit of excellence."

- Michael Jordan

What is it about a group of athletes running up and down a court, dribbling a ball, and soaring through the air to score that ignites the passion and excitement of basketball fans? To the uninitiated, it may seem like a simple game, but those who have experienced the magic of basketball understand its power to captivate, inspire, and create unforgettable moments. In the realm of basketball, there have been countless amazing events that have left an indelible mark on the sport and its fans.

In this collection of basketball's most amazing events, we will delve into a world of awe-inspiring performances, jaw-dropping plays, and historical moments that have shaped the game we know and love today. Each event has been carefully selected based on its significance, impact, and ability to showcase the incredible talents and athleticism of the players involved.

As you embark on this journey through basketball history, you will witness extraordinary displays of skill, determination, and clutch performances that have etched themselves into the collective memory of basketball enthusiasts worldwide. From the iconic shots that sealed championships to the fierce rivalries that intensified competition, these events embody the essence of the game and remind us why basketball continues to captivate audiences year after year.

The contents of this compilation have been meticulously ranked and organized to provide a comprehensive exploration of the most amazing events in basketball. We will take you through various chapters, each focusing on a specific theme or era, highlighting the incredible moments that define it. Whether you're a die-hard basketball fan or simply someone who appreciates the artistry and drama of the game, there is something for everyone within these pages.

In the first chapter, we will delve into the realm of buzzer-beaters and game-winning shots. These moments hang in the balance, where the outcome of the game rests on a single shot. You will relive the tension, the anticipation, and the exhilaration as players rise to the occasion and deliver in the most critical moments. From Michael Jordan's iconic "Flu Game" shot to Ray Allen's clutch three-pointer in the 2013 NBA Finals, these shots have become part of basketball lore, forever etched in the annals of the sport.

We will explore the era of dominant dynasties and legendary teams. Here, you will witness the unparalleled greatness of teams like the 1995-1996 Chicago Bulls and the 1980s "Showtime" Los Angeles Lakers. We will recount their triumphs, their rivalries, and the iconic moments that defined their reigns. From Magic Johnson's no-look passes to Scottie Pippen's defensive prowess, these teams showcased basketball at its finest, leaving an indelible mark on the sport and inspiring future generations of players.

Another chapter will take you on a journey through the storied history of basketball's greatest rivalries. From the fierce battles between Larry Bird's Boston Celtics and Magic Johnson's Los Angeles Lakers to the epic clashes between the Boston Celtics and the Los Angeles Lakers in the 1980s, these rivalries transcended the sport and became cultural touchstones. You will witness the intensity, the emotion, and the unwavering determination of players as they face off in pursuit of glory, leaving an enduring legacy that has shaped the fabric of basketball.

We will also delve into the realm of individual brilliance, celebrating the remarkable achievements of basketball's greatest players. From Wilt Chamberlain's 100-point game to Kobe Bryant's legendary 81-point performance, these transcendent displays of talent pushed the boundaries of what was deemed possible on a basketball court. You will witness the sheer dominance, skill, and artistry of these athletes as they etched their names in the record books and solidified their places in basketball history.

This collection will give you a deeper appreciation for the rich tapestry of basketball's most amazing events. You will witness the game's evolution from its humble beginnings to today's global phenomenon. Each chapter will transport you to a different era, immersing you in the sights, sounds, and emotions that defined that particular time in basketball history.

But beyond the sheer entertainment value, these amazing events hold deeper significance. They serve as reminders of the resilience, determination, and human spirit that basketball embodies. They inspire us to push ourselves beyond our limits, to believe in the power of teamwork, and to never underestimate the impact of a single moment.

As you journey through these pages, you will witness the stories behind the events, the narratives that unfolded, and the impact they had on the players, teams, and the sport as a whole. You will gain insights into the strategies, rivalries, and personalities that shaped these moments, revealing the intricate tapestry of basketball's history.

These amazing events are not just a walk down memory lane; it is an opportunity to learn, to reflect, and to be inspired.

Whether you are a young fan discovering the game's legends or a seasoned enthusiast revisiting cherished memories, there is something to be gained from each story shared within these pages.

By the end of this journey, you will have a deeper understanding of the beauty and allure of basketball. You will appreciate the countless hours of practice; the sacrifices made, and the sheer passion that drives players to reach new heights. You will gain a renewed admiration for the athletes who have left an indelible mark on the sport, forever etched in the hearts of fans worldwide.

So, as we explore basketball's most amazing events, let us relish in the game's magic. Let us celebrate the extraordinary moments, the transcendent performances, and the indomitable spirit that have shaped basketball into the global phenomenon it is today. And let us remember that beyond the game itself; it is the stories, the emotions, and the shared experiences that truly make basketball a universal language, connecting fans from all walks of life.

Now, let us turn our attention to the first chapter of this collection, where we will delve into the realm of buzzer-beaters and game-winning shots. Prepare to be on the edge of your seat as we relive the electrifying moments that have defined the essence of basketball drama. From the iconic shots reverberating through arenas to the hearts of fans, we invite you to join us on this exhilarating journey through the annals of basketball history.As the clock ticks down and the game hangs in the balance, these moments remind us why we love the game. So, witness the sheer magic of basketball's most amazing events. Let the journey begin.

THE MIRACLE ON ICE COURT

The Story of Kobe Bryant and the 2008 Beijing Olympics

"I have nothing in common with lazy people who blame others for their lack of success. Great things come from hard work and perseverance. No excuses."

- Kobe Bryant

Basketball legends go beyond the game. Many consider basketball players gods because of their physical strength and athletic ability. Their skill, determination, and relentless pursuit of greatness have immortalized her in the hearts of her fans. One name that stands out among these legends is the late great Kobe Bryant. One of Bryant's greatest stories is his incredible journey at the 2008 Beijing Olympics, forever known as the "Ice Rink Miracle."

A name that will forever be synonymous with greatness (and also not passing the ball on the court), Kobe Bryant achieved legendary status through his relentless pursuit of excellence. His unmatched skill and work ethic have made him one of the greatest basketball players ever. The 2008 Beijing Olympics set the stage for his most famous performance, cementing his legendary status and inspiring audiences worldwide.

The time is 2008; the Beijing Olympics should captivate the world with its scale and fierce competition. With this in mind, basketball tournaments promise to be battlegrounds for the best athletes in the world. This would be a chance for those who want to be great to prove themselves great. These Olympics brought many top athletes onto the international stage, including Usain Bolt, a legendary Jamaican runner. Kobe Bryant, already having made a name for himself on his home team, entered the tournament with only one goal in mind.

As a United States Men's Basketball Team member, Kobe Bryant's performance throughout the tournament was exceptional. Displaying unparalleled skill, unwavering determination, and a burning desire to succeed, he left an indelible mark on the world stage. From the opening hints of the basketball competition, it was clear that Bryant was a force to be reckoned with. His unparalleled athleticism and relentless drive propel the US team forward, inspire his teammates, and wow fans worldwide. With his dynamic presence on the field, Bryant has established himself as a true master of the game, demonstrating a wide range of shooting, ball-handling, and defensive skills.

Bryant's offensive skills were displayed throughout the

tournament and kept basketball fans excited. When the time was running out against Australia, he clinched the win for his team with a spectacular jump shot past two defenders. The match showed his ability to shoot under pressure and change the game's course last minute.

Another memorable moment came during a match against his arch-enemy Spain. Known for his fierce competitiveness, Bryant faced off against his Los Angeles Lakers teammate, Spanish star Pau Gasol. With sheer determination, Bryant thrilled the crowd and wowed fans with his skill and versatility with an array of offensive moves, including lightning-fast crossovers and gravity-defying dunks.

Bryant's defensive prowess was equally remarkable. In a game against Greece, he showcased his renowned "Black Mamba" mentality, shutting down opposing players with relentless on-ball defense. With lightning-quick footwork and anticipation, he intercepted passes, swiped at the ball, and disrupted the opposing team's offensive rhythm. One unforgettable play saw him execute a spectacular chase-down block, soaring through the air to reject a lay-up attempt, leaving spectators amazed.

Moreover, Bryant's leadership and ability to elevate his teammates' performances were evident throughout the tournament. With his unwavering confidence and unwavering work ethic, he commanded the respect of his fellow players.

During timeouts, he passionately rallied his teammates, instilling a sense of belief and unity within the squad. This infectious energy translated into inspired performances from his teammates, as they fed off his competitive spirit and elevated their game to new heights.

Off the court, Bryant's sportsmanship and humility further endeared him to fans around the world. Despite his superstar status, he consistently respected his opponents, engaging in friendly exchanges and congratulating them on their achievements. His humility and grace in victory and defeat were a testament to his character and a shining example for aspiring basketball players and fans.

Bryant's performance during the 2008 Olympics was a tour de force that showcased his unparalleled skills, fierce competitiveness, and leadership qualities. His ability to dominate games on both ends of the court, deliver jaw-dropping plays, and inspire his teammates solidified his status as one of the greatest basketball players of his generation. For basketball fans, witnessing Kobe Bryant's masterful performances during the 2008 Olympics was an unforgettable experience, a testament to his enduring legacy and impact on the sport.

The event is known as "The Miracle on Ice Court" because it resembles the iconic victory the United States hockey team had against The Soviet Union team in 1980. At the time, the Soviet Union was known to be indomitable regarding ice sports. The game occurred on February 22, 1980, and the Soviet team was heavily favored to win. However, the American team, led by coach Herb Brooks, played with tremendous heart, determination, and a never-give-up attitude. Against all odds, they defeated the Soviet Union by 4-3. The victory was seen as a symbol of American resilience, teamwork, and the underdog's triumph. Bryant's victory in leading the American basketball team to win the Olympics brought back the same pride that the original "Miracle on Ice" did. The fact that he played exceptionally in every game made everyone realize that one player can change the fate of the entire team.

THE SHOT HEARD AROUND THE WORLD

The Legend of Michael Jordan and the 1998 NBA Finals

"I've missed over 9,000 shots in my career. I've lost almost 300 games. Twenty-six times I've been trusted to take the game-winning shot and missed. I've failed over and over and over again in my life. And that is why I succeed."

\- Michael Jordan

As the final showdown of the NBA season, the 1998 Finals promised a clash of titans, pitting the Chicago Bulls, led by the incomparable Michael Jordan, against the formidable Utah Jazz (a team that would make Michael Jordan famous on more than one occasion). Amidst the electrifying atmosphere and mounting anticipation, Jordan stood poised to etch his indelible mark on the game. In a series that would test his mettle and shape his legacy, the stage was set for a battle reverberating far beyond the basketball court's confines.

The series had been fiercely contested, each team showcasing its exceptional talent and tenacity. The series stood deadlocked at 2-2, and the pivotal Game 6 was to be played on the Jazz's home court at the Delta Center in Salt Lake City, Utah. The atmosphere crackled with anticipation as fans poured into the arena, aware that a momentous chapter in basketball history was about to unfold.

The opening tip showed that both teams were prepared to leave everything on the court. The game was fiercely competitive, with momentum shifting back and forth. The Jazz, led by their formidable duo of Karl Malone and John Stockton, pushed the Bulls to the brink, refusing to yield an inch. But the Bulls had a secret weapon, a player whose competitive fire burned brighter than ever—Michael Jordan.

Throughout the game, Jordan displayed his trademark grace, athleticism, and uncanny ability to rise to the occasion when it mattered most. With his aerial acrobatics, seemingly defying gravity, he delivered a mesmerizing array of high-flying dunks, fadeaway jumpers, and seemingly impossible shots. Time and time again, he demonstrated his ability to conjure moments of pure magic, leaving fans and opponents alike in awe of his mastery.

As the game entered its final moments, the tension reached its zenith. With only 41.9 seconds remaining, the score was tied at 86 apiece. The Bulls had possession, and the world watched, holding its breath in anticipation. Jordan, determined to seize the moment, orchestrated a masterful drive towards the basket. He bypassed defenders with a quick step and a burst of speed, soaring toward the hoop.

But the Jazz, renowned for their stout defense, converged on Jordan, denying him an easy path to the basket. Undeterred, Jordan instinctively rose into the air, suspended like a majestic bird. He extended his right arm in mid-flight, palming the ball with an iron grip. With a seemingly impossible degree of body control, he adjusted his release, soaring higher to avoid the outstretched arms of Jazz center Greg Ostertag.

Time seemed to stand still as the ball left Jordan's hand, its trajectory soaring toward the hoop. The eyes of the world locked onto the spherical leather as it gracefully sliced through the air. It seemed as if destiny held its breath, waiting for the outcome of this celestial ballet. And then, with a swish, the basketball pierced the net, setting off a deafening roar from the crowd.

The Delta Center erupted in pandemonium as the Bulls took an 88-86 lead with only 5.2 seconds remaining. The shot was nothing short of miraculous, a testament to Jordan's unparalleled skill and his unyielding determination to achieve greatness. In that instant, Jordan's legacy was etched in stone—an indomitable champion capable of transcending the boundaries of human potential.

But the game was not yet over. The Jazz had one final opportunity to respond: stave off defeat and force a Game 7. John Stockton, renowned for his clutch playmaking abilities, sprinted up the court and was determined to orchestrate one last offensive play for the Jazz. As the clock ticked down, Stockton unleashed a pass to his partner in crime, Karl Malone, who positioned himself near the baseline. Malone, known for his dominance in the paint, caught the ball and prepared for a potential game-tying shot.

However, the Bulls were not about to let history slip away. Sensing the moment's gravity, the Bulls' defense swarmed Malone, converging upon him like a pack of hungry wolves. Malone attempted to drive toward the basket in a split-second decision, but lurking in the shadows was Michael Jordan, a defensive maestro.

Jordan, renowned for his ability to disrupt opponents' plays, anticipated Malone's move, lunging forward with cat-like reflexes. In a stunning display of defensive prowess, he extended his hand, his fingertips grazing the basketball, dislodging it from Malone's grasp. The ball careened into the hands of a waiting Scottie Pippen, who secured the steal and clinched the victory for the Bulls.

As the final buzzer sounded, the significance of Jordan's "Shot Heard Around the World" reverberated throughout the basketball universe. It was more than a game-winning shot; it was a moment of transcendent brilliance, a culmination of Jordan's unwavering desire to achieve greatness. His legendary status soared to new heights, leaving an indelible mark on the sport and captivating the imagination of fans around the globe.

The shot symbolized Jordan's relentless pursuit of excellence, his ability to deliver under immense pressure, and his unwavering belief in his own abilities. It embodied his unrivaled combination of skill, athleticism, and mental fortitude, establishing him as the quintessential clutch performer. Jordan's impact extended beyond the confines of the basketball court, inspiring generations of aspiring athletes and leaving an enduring legacy that continues to shape the game today.

Beyond the immediate triumph of that shot, Jordan's performance throughout the 1998 NBA Finals was a testament to his will to win. He averaged 33.5 points per game during the series, displaying an uncanny ability to take over games and lead his team to victory. His leadership, both on and off the court, galvanized the Bulls. This instilled a sense of belief and confidence that permeated throughout the roster.

In the aftermath of the "Shot Heard Around the World," Jordan's impact on the game and his legacy as one of basketball's greatest players was firmly cemented. The shot transcended the boundaries of sport, becoming a cultural touchstone forever etched in the collective memory of basketball fans worldwide. It represented the pinnacle of Jordan's illustrious career, culminating in his unparalleled skill, unrivaled competitiveness, and relentless pursuit of excellence.

To this day, the "Shot Heard Around the World" remains a testament to the power of sports to captivate our hearts, inspire our spirits, and remind us of the boundless potential of human achievement. It serves as a reminder that greatness is not merely defined by a single shot or moment but by a lifetime of dedication, sacrifice, and unwavering belief in one's abilities. And in the case of Michael Jordan, his shot heard worldwide will forever reverberate as a symbol of basketball brilliance and a testament to the transformative power of sport.

THE DOUBLE-NICKEL GAME

How Michael Jordan Scored 55 Points Against the New York Knicks

"Michael Jordan's 55-point masterpiece against the New York Knicks was a mesmerizing display of basketball brilliance, leaving fans and opponents alike in awe. It was a performance for the ages, a testament to his unrivaled greatness."

- Magic Johnson

Michael Jordan's 55-point performance against the New York Knicks on March 28, 1995, stands as one of the most memorable and extraordinary individual scoring outbursts in NBA history. This iconic game showcased Jordan's unmatched scoring prowess, unparalleled skill set, and relentless competitive spirit. From start to finish, Jordan delivered a virtuoso performance that left fans and opponents alike in awe, etching his name deeper into the annals of basketball greatness.

The stage was set at Madison Square Garden, the historic arena that had witnessed countless legendary performances. The Chicago Bulls, led by their fearless leader Michael Jordan, traveled to New York City to face their long-time rivals, the New York Knicks. This matchup was always intense and highly anticipated, as both teams had a storied history of fierce battles and bitter rivalries.

As the game began, it was clear that Jordan had a special fire burning within him. He relentlessly attacked the Knicks' defense, displaying his trademark combination of athleticism, finesse, and unparalleled basketball IQ. He seemed to weave through defenders effortlessly with each possession, gliding to the basket for acrobatic layups or rising above defenders for mid-range jumpers.

Jordan established his dominance from the outset, scoring at will and electrifying the crowd with his explosive moves. His sheer scoring ability was on full display as he effortlessly converted jump shots from various spots on the floor, showcasing his deadly mid-range game. The Knicks' defenders, known for their physicality and toughness, were left grasping at air as Jordan seemingly defied gravity, making the game look effortless.

As the game progressed, Jordan's scoring spree intensified. He found his rhythm, connecting on shot after shot, displaying an almost supernatural ability to anticipate defensive schemes and exploit even the slightest defensive lapses. Despite their best efforts, the Knicks were helpless in containing the basketball virtuoso, who seemed to be in a league of his own.

Jordan's scoring barrage reached its crescendo in the fourth quarter. With the game hanging in the balance, he elevated his play to an even higher level, displaying a killer instinct that defined his career. His every move exuded confidence, unleashing an array of mesmerizing scoring displays, leaving fans and onlookers awestruck. The Madison Square Garden crowd, notorious for their fervent support of the home team, soon found themselves caught between loyalty to the Knicks and an overwhelming admiration for the greatness they were witnessing. Each breathtaking move forced them to acknowledge Jordan's brilliance, even if it meant cheering for the opponent.

As the game clock ticked, the Bulls trailed by a narrow margin. But in true Jordan fashion, he embraced the pressure and took matters into his own hands. With an unwavering determination to secure victory, he launched a series of impossible shots, each finding the bottom of the net with surgical precision. His signature moment came with less than a minute remaining in the game. With the Bulls down by one point, Jordan received the ball on the wing, guarded tightly by John Starks, one of the league's most tenacious defenders. The arena held its collective breath as Jordan surveyed the situation with a calm yet focused expression.

With a swift jab step to create separation, Jordan rose into the air, his body perfectly aligned, and released a textbook-perfect jump shot. The ball soared through the air, spinning precisely, and gracefully swished through the net. The crowd erupted in disbelief and admiration as the Bulls reclaimed the lead.

But Jordan wasn't finished. He relentlessly attacked the basket in the final moments, drawing fouls and sinking clutch free throws to seal the victory. When the final buzzer sounded, the scoreboard displayed a remarkable statistic—Michael Jordan had scored a staggering 55 points, single-handedly carrying his team to a hard-fought victory over the Knicks.

The aftermath of Jordan's 55-point masterpiece was a testament to his transcendent greatness. The basketball world erupted with awe and admiration for the performance they had just witnessed. Fans, fellow players, coaches, and analysts marveled at Jordan's ability to elevate his game to extraordinary heights.

The 55-point explosion against the Knicks further solidified Jordan's status as the premier scorer of his era and perhaps in the sport's history. It showcased his unparalleled ability to take over a game and impose his will on both court ends. In that single game, he displayed a complete arsenal of offensive skills, combining relentless drives to the basket, smooth mid-range jumpers, and clutch shooting from beyond the arc.

But it wasn't just Jordan's scoring that made the performance legendary—it was the manner in which he did it. Jordan's game was characterized by an unyielding competitive spirit, a hunger for greatness that drove him to push his limits and surpass expectations. He thrived in pressure-packed situations, displaying a mental fortitude that elevated his performance when it mattered most.

The 55-point outburst against the Knicks also underscored Jordan's ability to rise against tough opponents. The Knicks, known for their physical and hard-nosed style of play, were renowned for their defensive prowess. Yet, Jordan found ways to dissect their defense, exploit their weaknesses, and leave them in his wake. It was a testament to his basketball IQ, ability to read the game, and relentless drive to overcome any challenge.

Beyond the individual accolades and the awe-inspiring point total, Jordan's performance against the Knicks showcased his leadership and ability to inspire his teammates. Throughout the game, he led by example, exhibiting a level of determination and intensity that was infectious. His teammates fed off his energy, raising their own performance to match his level of excellence.

Jordan's 55-point performance against the Knicks became a legend in the following years. It was etched into the collective memory of basketball fans as one of the defining moments of his career. It served as a reminder of his unmatched scoring ability, uncanny clutch performances, and unrelenting pursuit of victory.

The game added to Michael Jordan's enduring legacy as the best basketball player the world has ever seen.His impact on the sport extended far beyond the box or final scoreline. He revolutionized the game, inspiring a generation of players to strive for greatness, to push their limits, and to redefine what was possible on the basketball court.

In the pantheon of Jordan's illustrious career, the 55-point performance against the New York Knicks occupies a special place. It represents a microcosm of his greatness—the ability to rise to the occasion, to dominate in the face of adversity, and to leave an indelible mark on the sport. It was a game for the ages, a display of basketball brilliance that will forever be remembered as one of the most exceptional individual performances in the history of the NBA.

THE LOB CITY ERA

The Exciting Story of the Los Angeles Clippers' High-Flying Team

"Shoot for the moon, even if you miss, you'll land among the stars."

- Les Brown

In professional basketball, few teams have experienced as dramatic a transformation as the Los Angeles Clippers. Once regarded as a perennial underdog, the team emerged from the shadows to become one of the most exhilarating and captivating squads in the NBA. This is the story of how the Los Angeles Clippers' high-flying team captured the hearts of fans and redefined their franchise's identity.

The journey began in the early 2010s when the Clippers underwent a dramatic change in ownership. Under the guidance of new owner Steve Ballmer, the team sought to redefine itself on and off the court. Ballmer's infectious enthusiasm and unwavering commitment to success injected renewed energy into the organization, setting the stage for a remarkable transformation.

One of the pivotal moments in this journey occurred during the 2011–2012 season when the Clippers acquired two transcendent talents—Chris Paul and Blake Griffin. Paul, a masterful playmaker and floor general, brought a level of leadership and basketball IQ that the team had sorely lacked. On the other hand, Griffin possessed an unparalleled combination of size, strength, and athleticism, making him a force to be reckoned with on the court.

With Paul and Griffin at the helm, the Clippers embarked on a quest to shed their reputation as a perennially struggling franchise. The duo's chemistry quickly became apparent as they connected on alley-oop dunks and electrifying plays that sent shockwaves through the league. Their on-court partnership blossomed, captivating fans with their gravity-defying acrobatics and jaw-dropping displays of athleticism.

As the Clippers' high-flying style of play took shape, they quickly became known for their highlight-reel dunks, alley-oops, and fast-paced transition offense. Staples Center, their home arena, became a mecca of basketball entertainment, with fans eagerly anticipating the next gravity-defying dunk from Griffin or the precision passing of Paul.

The "Lob City" era was born, defined by their fearless attack on the rim and a commitment to exciting, fast-paced basketball.

Lob passes became a trademark of the team's offensive strategy, as Paul's impeccable court vision allowed him to thread the needle with pinpoint accuracy. Griffin, known for his awe-inspiring leaping ability, elevated the art of finishing at the rim to new heights, consistently mesmerizing crowds with his thunderous slams.

But the Clippers' transformation was not solely attributed to their dynamic duo. The team's supporting cast was integral to their rise to prominence. DeAndre Jordan, a defensive stalwart and dominant rebounder, anchored the paint with his shot-blocking prowess and tenaciousness on the glass. Jamal Crawford, the team's prolific sixth man, provided instant offense and a scoring spark off the bench, captivating fans with his silky-smooth shooting and clutch performances.

Under the guidance of head coach Doc Rivers, the Clippers developed a winning culture and an unbreakable bond. Rivers instilled a sense of unity and accountability within the team, fostering a winning mentality that translated onto the court. The players embraced their roles, sacrificing personal statistics for the team's success. The culture of camaraderie and resilience became the foundation of the Clippers' newfound success.

With each passing season, the Clippers continued to ascend, solidifying themselves as a force to be reckoned with in the NBA. They routinely found themselves among the league's elite, competing for division titles and making deep playoff runs. The electrifying performances and high-flying exploits of the team earned them widespread recognition and a growing legion of devoted fans.

The Clippers' journey was not without its share of challenges and heartbreak. They faced formidable adversaries and grueling postseason battles, often falling agonizingly short of their ultimate goal. But through the adversity, the team remained resilient and determined, using each setback as fuel to push harder and strive for greatness.

One of the defining moments in the Clippers' rise to prominence came during the 2019–2020 season. The team boldly moved by adding another superstar to their roster—Kawhi Leonard, a two-time NBA champion and Finals MVP. Leonard brought a quiet intensity and a relentless work ethic that perfectly complemented the team's identity. His stoic demeanor and clutch performances added a new dimension to the Clippers' formidable arsenal.

With Leonard joining forces with Paul, Griffin, and the rest of the roster, the Clippers assembled a "Big Three" that sent shockwaves through the league. The team's high-flying style of play reached new heights as Leonard showcased his incredible scoring ability, Paul orchestrated the offense with precision, and Griffin astounded with his aerial acrobatics. The Staples Center became an arena of anticipation as fans eagerly awaited the next highlight-reel moment.

The Clippers showcased their dominance as the regular season unfolded, securing a top seed in the Western Conference. Their electrifying performances became the talk of the league, and the basketball world took notice of their emergence as a legitimate championship contender. The stage was set for a postseason run that could solidify their place in NBA history.

However, the 2020 NBA playoffs brought unexpected challenges and a heartbreaking twist of fate. The Clippers were commanding in a highly anticipated Western Conference semifinal matchup against the Denver Nuggets, leading the series 3-1. But as the basketball gods would have it, the Nuggets mounted a historic comeback, winning three consecutive games to eliminate the Clippers from the playoffs.

The defeat was a bitter pill for the Clippers and their fans. The dream of a championship had slipped through their fingers, leaving them disappointed. But true to their resilient nature, the Clippers refused to let the setback define them. They vowed to learn from their mistakes, regroup, and return stronger the following season.

The legacy of the Los Angeles Clippers' high-flying team extends far beyond their on-court exploits. They symbolize the power of resilience, the triumph of perseverance, and the ability to captivate an entire fanbase with their electrifying style of play. Their journey is a testament to the transformative power of teamwork, dedication, and unwavering belief in a shared vision.

As the Clippers continue to chase their championship aspirations, their high-flying style of play and indomitable spirit resonate with fans worldwide. They have redefined what it means to be a Clippers fan, instilling a sense of pride and excitement that was once unimaginable. The journey is far from over, and the Clippers remain poised to etch their names in basketball history with their relentless pursuit of excellence.

Ultimately, the story of the Los Angeles Clippers' high-flying team is one of redemption, resilience, and the unbreakable bond between a city and its beloved basketball team. It is a story of defying expectations, soaring to new heights, and inspiring a generation of fans with breathtaking athleticism and unwavering determination. The Clippers' journey is a reminder that sometimes the most exciting stories in sports are not only about championships won but also the indomitable spirit that keeps us coming back for more.

THE DREAM TEAM

The Amazing Journey of the 1992 United States Men's Olympic Basketball Team

"Greatness is not found in possessions, power, position, or prestige; it is discovered in goodness, humility, service, and character."

- Michael Jordan

There are few teams in history as iconic and dominant as the 1992 United States Men's Olympic Basketball Team. Composed of some of the greatest players ever to grace the hardcourt, the "Dream Team" captivated the world with their unrivaled talent, sheer dominance, and unyielding pursuit of excellence. This is the story of the amazing journey of the 1992 United States Men's Olympic Basketball Team.

The stage was set for the Dream Team's journey at the 1992 Summer Olympics held in Barcelona, Spain. The United States, in an unprecedented move, assembled a roster of basketball legends that included Michael Jordan, Magic Johnson, Larry Bird, Charles Barkley, Scottie Pippen, Karl Malone, Patrick Ewing, David Robinson, and many others. Coached by the legendary Chuck Daly, the team was a veritable "who's who" of basketball greatness.

From the moment the Dream Team stepped on the Olympic stage, they were overwhelmed with anticipation and excitement. Fans from all corners of the globe flocked to witness the spectacle of this star-studded team in action. The media frenzy surrounding the Dream Team was unprecedented, as the world awaited their every move, both on and off the court.

It wasn't just the star power that made the Dream Team special; it was the unity and camaraderie that existed among these basketball titans. Despite their individual achievements and superstar status, the players embraced their roles and selflessly put the team above all else. Mutual respect and admiration permeated the locker room, creating a cohesive unit capable of achieving greatness.

The Dream Team's journey began with a series of exhibition games leading up to the Olympics. These exhibitions served as a preview of the basketball spectacle that awaited the world. With each game, the team's chemistry and dominance became increasingly evident. They dismantled opponents with breathtaking displays of skill, precision passing, and electrifying dunks that left audiences in awe.

As the Olympic tournament commenced, the Dream Team continued their reign of basketball supremacy. Their opponents were in awe; their countries' best players were overmatched and overwhelmed by the sheer talent and skill of the American squad. Game after game, the Dream Team unleashed a brand of basketball that transcended the sport itself. They made the impossible seem routine, executing flawless fast breaks, alley-oop dunks, and three-point barrages that defied logic.

Beyond the dazzling displays of individual brilliance, the Dream Team's success was a testament to their exceptional teamwork and strategic execution. The players seamlessly blended their diverse skill sets, playing off each other's strengths and elevating the level of play. Their selflessness and unselfishness were evident in every pass, every screen, and every defensive rotation.

Off the court, the Dream Team's impact extended far beyond the game itself. They served as global ambassadors of basketball, spreading the sport's popularity to every corner of the world. Their presence in Barcelona created a basketball fever that swept through the city, inspiring a new generation of players and fans.

Moreover, the Dream Team's journey symbolized a historic moment in basketball history. It represented a turning point in the globalization of the sport as the NBA's influence expanded beyond American borders. The team's presence and dominance showcased the level of talent in the United States, solidifying the country's basketball prowess on the international stage.

As the tournament progressed, it became clear that the Dream Team was on a path to ultimate glory. They easily advanced through the knockout stages, leaving a trail of defeated opponents in their wake. And in the gold medal game, the Dream Team faced Croatia, a formidable opponent led by future NBA star Dražen Petrović. The gold medal clash was highly anticipated, pitting two talented teams against each other in a battle for Olympic supremacy.

The gold medal game showcased the Dream Team's exceptional skill and dominance. Led by the scoring prowess of Michael Jordan, who poured in a game-high 22 points, the United States asserted their authority from the opening tip-off. The team's suffocating defense and high-octane offense overwhelmed Croatia, as they built a commanding lead and never looked back.

But the game was not just about the final score; it celebrated basketball at its finest. The Dream Team's display of individual brilliance, teamwork, and sportsmanship had a lasting impact on the sport. They exhibited a level of basketball artistry rarely witnessed, blending precision, creativity, and sheer athleticism to create a spectacle that transcended the game.

As the final buzzer sounded, the Dream Team had secured an emphatic victory, capturing the gold medal with a resounding 117-85 triumph. The players embraced in joy and relief, knowing they had accomplished something special. They had fulfilled not only their own dreams but also the dreams of millions of basketball fans worldwide.

The Dream Team's journey did not end with the gold medal. Their impact reverberated throughout the basketball landscape for years to come. Their style of play, marked by an emphasis on team basketball, unselfishness, and showmanship, influenced a generation of players who aspired to emulate their greatness.

The Dream Team's legacy extended far beyond the Olympics. Their presence and dominance inspired a renewed interest in basketball worldwide. The international game underwent a transformation, with more countries investing in their basketball programs and producing a new wave of talented players. The Dream Team's influence opened doors for athletes from all over the globe to compete at the highest level, making basketball a truly global phenomenon.

Individually, the players of the Dream Team cemented their legacies as basketball icons. Michael Jordan solidified his status as the greatest player of his generation, further enhancing his basketball immortality. Magic Johnson and Larry Bird, already legends in their own right, added another chapter to their storied careers. And the younger stars like Charles Barkley, Karl Malone, and Scottie Pippen elevated their profiles and went on to have illustrious careers in the NBA.

The impact of the Dream Team extended beyond their own

success. Their triumph ignited a renewed interest in basketball in the United States, leading to a surge in popularity and television ratings for the NBA. The league experienced a golden era in the 1990s, with fan attendance and global viewership reaching unprecedented levels.

The story of the 1992 United States Men's Olympic Basketball Team, the Dream Team, is a tale of basketball excellence, camaraderie, and global impact. Their journey captivated the world, leaving an indelible mark on the sport and inspiring generations of players and fans. They exemplified the true spirit of teamwork, showcasing that the possibilities are limitless when extraordinary talent comes together.

The Dream Team's amazing journey was not just about winning games and collecting gold medals; it was about the power of sport to transcend borders, unite nations, and inspire greatness. They represented the pinnacle of basketball achievement and forever etched their names in the annals of sports history. The Dream Team's legacy will continue to inspire basketball players and fans for generations, reminding us of the transformative power of dreams, teamwork, and the pursuit of excellence.

THE FLU GAME

How Michael Jordan Led the Chicago Bulls to Victory Despite Being Sick

---

"Obstacles don't have to stop you. If you run into a wall, don't turn around and give up. Figure out how to climb it, go through it, or work around it."

- Michael Jordan

Facing off against the Utah Jazz in a crucial Game 5, Jordan defied the odds and led the Chicago Bulls to victory despite battling a severe illness. This is the remarkable story of Michael Jordan, showcasing his indomitable spirit, determination, and sheer willpower to inspire his team and secure a pivotal win against his constant nemesis, Utah Jazz (who inadvertently keep leading him to further greatness).

The stage was set on June 11, 1997, at the Delta Center in Salt Lake City. The Chicago Bulls, seeking their fifth NBA championship in seven years, were locked in a grueling battle with the formidable Utah Jazz. The series was tied at 2-2, and Game 5 held immense significance, as it often determined the trajectory of a series.

But little did anyone know that this game would go down in history as one of Michael Jordan's most heroic performances. Hours before tip-off, Jordan fell ill with what was initially diagnosed as a severe case of the flu. He was weak, fatigued, and battling a high fever. The circumstances appeared dire, and many questioned whether he could even suit up for the game.

Yet, true to his competitive nature and unwavering commitment to his team, Jordan refused to let his illness dictate the game's outcome. He summoned every ounce of strength and determination to lead the Bulls onto the court, knowing his presence alone would boost his teammates psychologically.

As the game commenced, it became evident that Jordan's illness had affected his physical abilities. His movements were noticeably slower, and his normally explosive athleticism seemed diminished. But what he lacked in physical prowess, he more than compensated for with his mental fortitude, basketball IQ, and sheer force of will.

Jordan pushed through the fatigue, battling against a relentless opponent and his body's limitations. With every step, he displayed an unrivaled level of focus and mental toughness, refusing to let his illness define him or hinder his ability to impact the game. It was as if his determination created an invisible shield, shielding him from the debilitating effects of his condition.

The Bulls found themselves locked in a fierce battle against the Jazz as the game progressed. Fueled by their home crowd, Utah mounted a relentless offensive attack, seeking to take advantage of Jordan's weakened state. But Jordan, despite his physical limitations, rose to the occasion time and time again, providing a masterclass in leadership and clutch play.

With each possession, Jordan dug deep into his reserves, drawing on his vast repertoire of offensive moves and uncanny ability to read the game. He scored from all areas of the court, hitting mid-range jumpers, driving to the basket, and even knocking down crucial three-pointers. Each shot was a testament to his mental strength and unwavering belief that he could lead his team to victory.

But Jordan's impact extended beyond his scoring prowess. He orchestrated the Bulls' offense precisely, making timely passes and creating scoring opportunities for his teammates. Despite his weakened state, his court vision remained razor-sharp, allowing him to exploit defensive gaps and find open shooters. His ability to elevate the play of his teammates, even in the face of adversity, demonstrated his unparalleled leadership and ability to inspire those around him.

The game climaxed in the fourth quarter, with both teams in a back-and-forth battle. The Jazz, smelling an opportunity to seize the series, threw everything they had at the resilient Bulls. But Jordan, fueled by an inner fire that burned brighter than ever, rose to the challenge and delivered when it mattered most.

In the game's final minutes, with the score tied and the outcome hanging in the balance, Jordan summoned his last energy reserves and made a series of remarkable plays that would etch his name in basketball folklore.

With less than a minute remaining, Jordan, visibly exhausted but refusing to back down, drove to the basket with determination. Despite the Jazz's best efforts to impede him, he defied gravity, contorting his body mid-air and releasing a layup that found its mark. The crowd erupted in disbelief as the Bulls took the lead.

But Jordan wasn't finished yet. He demonstrated his defensive prowess on the ensuing defensive possession by stripping the ball from Jazz guard Karl Malone, preventing a potential game-winning score. The play showcased his offensive brilliance and tenacity, and ability to make a difference on both court ends.

As the final seconds ticked away, Jordan stepped to the free-throw line with the weight of the game on his shoulders. With fatigue etched on his face, he calmly sank both free throws, extending the Bulls' lead and effectively sealing the victory. It was a testament to his mental strength and unwavering focus as he blocked out the noise, the illness, and the pressure to deliver under the brightest of spotlights.

The final buzzer sounded, and the Bulls emerged victorious, winning the game 90-88. Jordan's heroic performance, despite being sick, left an indelible mark on the collective consciousness of basketball fans worldwide. His ability to rise above adversity, to defy the limitations imposed by illness, and to lead his team to victory was a testament to his unrivaled greatness.

The "Flu Game" solidified Jordan's legacy as one of the greatest basketball players of all time and symbolized inspiration and perseverance. It embodied the relentless pursuit of excellence, the unwavering commitment to one's craft, and the ability to summon extraordinary strength when it matters most.

Beyond the individual accolades, Jordan's performance in the "Flu Game" showcased the power of a leader to uplift and inspire those around him. His teammates, witnessing his unparalleled determination and resilience, drew strength from his example. They rallied around him, recognizing that they were part of something truly extraordinary.

The "Flu Game" epitomized the competitive fire within Jordan. It manifested his unyielding desire to win, regardless of the circumstances. His unwillingness to accept defeat, even when faced with significant obstacles, exemplified his unparalleled drive and competitiveness.

The "Flu Game" would become legendary in the years that followed. It would be recounted in countless basketball discussions, etched in fans' memories, and serve as a reminder of the immense impact one player can have on the outcome of a game. It would be cited as a prime example of Jordan's unrivaled greatness and his mark on the sport.

But beyond fame and recognition, the "Flu Game" shows the strength of the human spirit. It displayed the power of determination, resilience, and the refusal to let circumstances dictate one's destiny. It inspired countless athletes in basketball and all walks of life to push past their limitations and strive for greatness.

THE MALICE AT THE PALACE

The Shocking Brawl Between the Detroit Pistons and Indiana Pacers

"The ultimate measure of a man is not where he stands in moments of comfort and convenience, but where he stands at times of challenge and controversy."

- Martin Luther King Jr.

Not every major event in basketball has been a positive one, but the most important thing has always been the event's outcome. In the history of professional sports, few events have captured the attention of fans and the media, quite like the shocking brawl that unfolded on November 19, 2004 The incident between the Detroit Pistons and Indiana Pacers, which has since been dubbed "Malice at the Palace," sent shockwaves through the NBA and forever altered the perception of player-fan interactions.

The stage was set at the Palace of Auburn Hills, the home arena of the Detroit Pistons. The game between the Pistons and the Pacers was a highly anticipated matchup featuring two of the league's most physical and competitive teams. The rivalry between the two franchises had been simmering for years, fueled by previous playoff encounters and mutual disdain.

As the game progressed, tensions reached a boiling point. With less than a minute remaining in the fourth quarter and the Pacers holding a commanding lead, a hard foul by the Pistons' Ben Wallace on the Pacers' Ron Artest ignited the powder keg. Artest took exception to the foul and immediately confronted Wallace, leading to a shoving match between the two players.

The altercation between Wallace and Artest quickly escalated into an all-out brawl as players from both teams rushed to join the fray. Punches were thrown, bodies collided, and chaos ensued on the court. The referees struggled to regain control of the situation, but their efforts proved futile as the fighting spilled over into the stands.

Amidst the mayhem, Ron Artest, now known as Metta World Peace, retreated to the scorer's table, lying down to calm himself. However, a fan seated courtside decided to take matters into his own hands. He threw a drink at Artest, striking him square in the chest. In an instant, all restraint was lost, and Artest charged into the stands, followed closely by several other players.

What unfolded next was a scene of utter chaos. Players, coaches, and security personnel desperately tried to separate the combatants as punches were thrown, and fans fought back in self-defense. The atmosphere inside The Palace of Auburn Hills shifted from a place of competition and entertainment to one of sheer pandemonium and danger.

The brawl lasted for several minutes before order was eventually restored. The consequences of the melee were severe and far-reaching. Nine players were suspended, totaling 146 games, with Ron Artest receiving the harshest penalty of the season-long suspension. Five fans were also charged with criminal offenses for their involvement in the incident.

The "Malice at the Palace" fallout extended well beyond the suspensions and legal proceedings. The NBA was forced to confront the issue of player-fan interactions head-on, implementing new security measures and stricter codes of conduct. The incident served as a wake-up call for the league, highlighting the need for a safer and more respectful environment for players and fans alike.

The brawl also had lasting implications for the players involved. Ron Artest, who bore the brunt of the blame for his actions, underwent a personal transformation in the aftermath of the incident. He worked on improving his emotional stability and advocated for mental health awareness. Metta World Peace emerged as a different person, committed to using his platform to spread positivity and make a difference in the community.

Furthermore, "Malice at the Palace" forever changed the perception of the Detroit Pistons and Indiana Pacers franchises.

Both teams faced public scrutiny and were seen as aggressors in the incident. It took years for the organizations to rebuild their reputations and regain the trust of fans and sponsors.

In the broader context of the NBA, the brawl served as a stark reminder of the importance of sportsmanship, self-control, and the need to maintain professionalism on and off the court. The incident prompted soul-searching within the league and sparked discussions about the role of player behavior, fan conduct, and the responsibility of all parties involved in maintaining a respectful and safe environment.

"Malice at the Palace" became a defining moment in NBA history, not only for its shocking nature but also for its lasting impact on the sport. It forced the league to reevaluate its security protocols, fan engagement strategies, and disciplinary measures. The incident served as a catalyst for change, leading to stricter enforcement of rules and regulations to prevent such incidents from occurring in the future.

The fallout from the brawl also shed light on the complex dynamics between players and fans. It prompted a broader conversation about the boundaries between athletes and spectators and the need for mutual respect and understanding. Fans were reminded that their involvement in the game, while passionate, should never cross the line into violence or hostility. Similarly, players were urged to maintain composure and restraint, even in the face of provocation or intense emotions.

In the years following the "Malice at the Palace," the NBA took significant steps to enhance the fan experience and promote a more positive atmosphere during games. Initiatives such as increased security presence, stricter enforcement of fan conduct policies, and educational campaigns to foster mutual respect between players and fans were implemented league-wide. These efforts aimed to ensure that the focus remained on the game itself, celebrating the athleticism and skill of the players rather than devolving into confrontations and altercations.

Moreover, the incident sparked a broader conversation about the role of professional athletes as role models and ambassadors for their respective sports. It reminded players of the influence they wield and the responsibility they bear in setting an example for younger generations. The incident served as a powerful reminder that athletes, as public figures, are held to higher standards of conduct and must strive to represent themselves, their teams, and the league with dignity and integrity.

In the aftermath of the "Malice at the Palace," the NBA experienced a period of introspection and transformation. The league and its players collectively worked to rebuild trust, restore the integrity of the game, and create an environment where sportsmanship and respect were paramount. The incident became a turning point in the league's history, spurring a renewed commitment to professionalism, accountability, and maintaining a positive image on and off the court.

As time has passed, the "Malice at the Palace" has become a cautionary tale, a reminder of the potential consequences when emotions run high and lines are crossed. It is a stark reminder of the need for restraint, self-control, and respect in professional sports. The incident continues to shape the NBA's approach to player-fan interactions, security measures, and the ongoing quest to maintain a harmonious and enjoyable experience for all involved.

THE UNSTOPPABLE STREAK

Wilt Chamberlain and the Philadelphia Warriors

"He's an unstoppable force on the basketball court. No one can contain him."

- Anon

It can be said that Wilt Chamberlain walked so that Michael Jordan could run. Achieving things that were never seen before, Chamberlain was and still is a force to be reckoned with. Leaving an indelible mark on basketball forever and etched into the hearts of true football fans. One of the most amazing feats that he ever managed to achieve was his dominance on the court in the 1960s which struck fear into his opponents' hearts whenever he entered the field.

Wilt Chamberlain holds the record that is still speculated never to be emulated again for scoring double-doubles. Having also been the only player in history to have scored a quintuple-double. In basketball, a double-double refers to a statistical achievement when a player accumulates double-digit numbers in two of the five major statistical categories during a single game. The five major statistical categories are typically points, rebounds, assists, steals, and blocks. However, the most common combination for a double-double in points and rebounds.

To achieve a double-double, a player must record at least ten or more in two of these categories. For example, a player who scores 15 points and grabs 12 rebounds in a game would have achieved a double-double. Similarly, a player who records 18 points and 10 assists would also have a double-double.

The points category represents the number of field goals made and free throws converted by a player during the game. Rebounds measure the number of times a player retrieves the ball after a missed shot, whether it's an offensive rebound (retrieving a missed shot from their team) or a defensive rebound (retrieving a missed shot from the opposing team).

Double-doubles are an important statistical achievement because they indicate a player's ability to contribute significantly in multiple areas of the game. It showcases their scoring ability, rebounding prowess, or their playmaking skills. Players who consistently record double-doubles are often key contributors to their teams and are highly regarded for their versatility and impact on the game.

It's worth noting that double-doubles are not limited to a

single game. Players can achieve double-doubles over a series of games or even maintain a streak of consecutive double-doubles, further solidifying their impact and consistency. The ability to consistently achieve double-doubles often indicates a player's skill, work ethic, and overall basketball prowess.

Double-doubles have become a common metric for evaluating players' performances and contributions to their teams. They serve as a recognition of a player's well-roundedness and ability to make a significant impact across multiple aspects of the game. Players who consistently achieve double-doubles often garner recognition, and accolades and are considered key contributors to their team's success.

Explaining all that was necessary because double-doubles becoming a measure of metric success is invaluable to the conversation of Chamberlain setting the record. Whenever he would enter the court, there was tension all around. The opposing team would wonder if today would be the day that Chamberlain's streak would finally end, and if it did, that would mean that it would be a momentous game that went down in history. The fans would sit at the edge of their seats, waiting for what would happen next. Even those opposing the team Chamberlain would be playing with would have a keen eye out to see what would happen.

This inevitably placed a lot of pressure on Chamberlain. Instead of cracking under all the pressure though, he chose to rise above it all and excel in every game that he played. He would send eternal shockwaves throughout the basketball community by attaining 968 double-doubles in his entire career, never missing a beat. He would score an average of 50 points per game. This is why many say that Wilt Chamberlain was a better player than Michael Jordan. He dominated the court like no other player has managed to since.

In Chamberlain's worst season, he averaged about twenty points per game which is honestly a pretty good season for the average and even good NBA basketball player. Many people speculate that the reason why many of Chamberlain's achievements are under-appreciated is that they were just so amazing and unfathomable that people mostly couldn't believe that they happened.

"We'd go into a dressing room and see a box score from the night before where Wilt had 55 or 60 points. No one would think twice about it. Getting 50-some points, or even 60-some, wasn't news when Wilt did it." Kevin Loughery, a former basketball player, would comment on Chamberlain's performance.

Chamberlain's streak ended on March 20, 1962, after an astonishing 62 games. Considered by many to be an inhuman feat of athleticism. His final stat line during the streak was nothing short of extraordinary, with an average of 48.5 points and 25.9 rebounds per game. These numbers still stand as some of the most remarkable in NBA history.

Even though his streak ended, its mark on the game can still be felt. Chamberlain left a goal so tough to beat that many wonder if it ever even happened. But Chamberlain was a man that proved that he was just conditioned to achieve the impossible. There's a saying that the bumble bee is scientifically proven to be too big to fly, but no one told the bumble bee that, so it just keeps flying. Chamberlain must be like the bumble bee, obviously, people told him he couldn't achieve certain things, but he chose not to listen, and right now still holds the record for the longest streak of achieving double-doubles in NBA history.

THE DUNK OF DEFIANCE

Vince Carter and the Toronto Raptors

"He defied gravity with that dunk! It's a moment that will be remembered for generations."

- a commentator on Vince Carter

Outside of hockey and other winter/water sports, Canada has never really gotten much attention for team sports, especially not in basketball. This play would be the turning point though, that would inspire basketball fans for generations after it happened.

When it comes to how countries are viewed, Canada has always been seen as the colder, less popular, and less talented version of the USA. So it was ingrained in people's minds that whenever a basketball match happened between American team and Canadian teams; it was natural that the American team would win. That was the climate that the Toronto Raptors were operating in. They were growing in popularity, but they still needed an event that would boost them to international star status. That event would be their match against the Houston Rockets.

It was a regular-season game between the Toronto Raptors and the Houston Rockets. The Air Canada Centre was buzzing with anticipation as fans eagerly awaited the clash between two talented teams. The spotlight, however, was firmly fixed on Vince Carter, an athletic marvel whose gravity-defying feats had captivated the basketball world.

The game was in full swing when the Raptors gained possession. Carter, always ready to ignite the crowd with his acrobatic prowess, sprinted down the court. The anticipation in the arena was palpable as fans rose to their feet, their eyes fixated on the young superstar.

With lightning speed and unparalleled agility, Carter found himself soaring toward the basket. It was a moment frozen in time, a convergence of athleticism and audacity. Rising above the defenders, Carter extended his arm, reaching back as if to harness the power of the heavens themselves. With one fluid motion, he unleashed a thunderous one-handed slam dunk.

Frédéric Weis, a 7-foot-2 defender for the Houston Rockets, became an unwitting participant in Carter's spectacle. As Carter descended from the stratosphere, Weis stood frozen, a mere bystander to an act of defiance against the constraints of physics. Carter's outstretched arm seemed to graze the clouds as he threw down the dunk with a ferocity that resonated through the arena.

The impact was immediate. The crowd erupted in a cacophony of cheers and applause, their collective roar reverberating through the stadium. At that moment, the Air Canada Centre became an electric cauldron of jubilation. Fans, overwhelmed by the sheer spectacle of Carter's dunk, could scarcely believe what they had witnessed.

The dunk of defiance was a transcendent moment, encapsulating the essence of Vince Carter's game. It epitomized his audacity to challenge the limits of what was considered possible in basketball. Carter was a force of nature, a player who defied gravity and expectations with every soaring leap.

Beyond the immediate spectacle, the dunk had far-reaching consequences. It became an iconic symbol, etching itself into the collective memory of sports fans worldwide. It represented the fusion of artistry and athleticism, a testament to the beauty of the game. Carter's dunk would forever be remembered as a moment that transcended the sport, inspiring generations of aspiring athletes to dream big and reach for the stars.

For the Toronto Raptors franchise, the dunk of defiance was a turning point. It ignited a newfound passion within the city, propelling the team to unprecedented heights. The Raptors became a team to be reckoned with, capturing the attention of fans and opponents alike. Carter's dunk put the Raptors on the basketball map, solidifying their place in the NBA landscape. It not only ignited a new passion in the city but became a source of inspiration for people all around Canada.

The impact of the dunk extended beyond the court. Vince Carter became a global basketball superstar, his name synonymous with awe-inspiring dunks and unparalleled athleticism. Fans across the world marveled at his raw talent and the audacity with which he approached the game. Carter's ability to captivate audiences with his breathtaking displays of athleticism endeared him to fans and secured his place in basketball lore. It was rare that a star basketball player came from somewhere other than America or Africa.

Amidst the sea of fans cheering for Vince Carter's Dunk of Defiance, there was one spectator whose reaction stood out among the rest. In the crowd, that day was a young boy named Michael, who had been battling a serious illness. Michael's love for basketball has been a constant source of joy and strength throughout his challenging journey.

Unbeknownst to Vince Carter, his dunk held a profound significance for Michael. The young boy had closely followed Carter's career and had been inspired by his resilience and determination on and off the court. The Dunk of Defiance became a symbol of hope and courage for Michael, a reminder that even in the face of adversity, dreams could be realized. It gave him the strength to conquer what he was going through. That's not the only instance when sports has been a catalyst to help people overcome their tribulations.

The dunk of defiance became a rallying cry for those who dared to challenge the status quo. It represented the triumph of the underdog, the ability to rise above expectations and break free from the shackles of convention. It became a symbol of empowerment and resilience, reminding individuals that they, too, could defy the limits imposed on them. It also became one way that Canadians could finally gloat (in a good-natured way) over their American counterparts because what's the point of sports if you can't poke fun at your opponents once in a while?

THE KING'S CORONATION

LeBron James and the Miami Heat

"Success is not defined by the challenges we face, but by our ability to rise above them. The Redemption Game taught us that with resilience and belief, even the greatest setbacks could become stepping stones to triumph."

- LeBron James

L eBron James, hailed as one of the greatest basketball players of all time, had experienced his fair share of ups and downs throughout his illustrious career. However, it was during the 2010-2011 NBA season that he faced one of the most significant challenges of his career. James had just joined the Miami Heat, forming a formidable trio alongside Dwyane Wade and Chris Bosh. The "Big Three" were expected to dominate the league and capture multiple championships.

The 2010-2011 season began with high expectations, but the Miami Heat stumbled out of the gate. Their performance fell short of the lofty standards set for them, and the team faced criticism from fans and media alike. LeBron James, in particular, bore the brunt of the backlash. His decision to leave his hometown team, the Cleveland Cavaliers, in pursuit of a championship had been met with resentment and disdain.

As the regular season progressed, the pressure on LeBron James intensified. The media scrutinized his every move, and his every mistake was magnified. The public perception of him shifted from admiration to skepticism. He was labeled as a player who couldn't handle the pressure, a superstar who shrank in the biggest moments.

The pinnacle of the season arrived with the NBA Finals. The Miami Heat faced off against the Dallas Mavericks, a team hungry for redemption after a bitter defeat in the previous year's Finals. The stage was set for an epic battle between two talented squads, but it was LeBron James who found himself under the brightest spotlight.

The series started poorly for James and the Heat. They fell behind early, losing the first two games on their home court. The media seized the opportunity to amplify the narrative of James' failures, fueling doubts about his ability to deliver when it mattered most. The pressure reached its peak as the series shifted to Dallas for Games 3, 4, and 5.

In Game 3, the Miami Heat desperately needed a win to avoid falling into a 3-0 series hole. LeBron James, burdened by the weight of expectations, took the court with a renewed focus. He played with a determination and intensity that ignited his teammates. James showcased his versatility, contributing in all facets of the game. He scored points, grabbed rebounds, facilitated the offense, and locked down defensively. It was a masterclass performance that silenced the doubters, at least temporarily.

The Miami Heat emerged victorious in Game 3, providing a glimmer of hope. However, Game 4 proved to be a setback, as they once again faltered in the face of adversity. The Dallas Mavericks displayed resilience and executed their game plan flawlessly, leaving the Heat in a precarious position. It was a humbling moment for LeBron James and the entire team, a realization that they had to dig deep and find a way to turn the tide.

As Game 5 approached, LeBron James found himself at a crossroads. He could succumb to the doubts and criticisms that plagued him or rise above the noise and redefine his narrative. In a pivotal game, he chose the latter.

Game 5 of the NBA Finals would become a defining moment in LeBron James' career. He unleashed a performance for the ages, a display of greatness that would etch his name in the annals of basketball history. From the opening tip-off, James dominated every facet of the game. He attacked the basket relentlessly, displaying an unmatched combination of power, finesse, and precision. He showcased his ability to score from all areas of the court, whether it be driving to the rim, knocking down mid-range jumpers, or draining clutch three-pointers. His basketball IQ was on full display as he made impeccable decisions, finding open teammates with pinpoint passes and orchestrating the offense with unrivaled vision.

Defensively, LeBron James was a force to be reckoned with. He disrupted passing lanes, swatted away shots, and anchored the Heat's defense with his imposing presence. His relentless effort and tenacity set the tone for the entire team, inspiring them to elevate their performance to new heights.

As the game unfolded, the Miami Heat surged ahead, fueled by LeBron James' brilliance. The atmosphere in the arena was electric, with fans on the edge of their seats, witnessing a basketball virtuoso in action. With every basket, assist, and defensive stop, James erased the doubts and silenced the naysayers. It was a performance that transcended statistics, as his impact on the game went far beyond the numbers on the scoreboard.

LeBron James secured the victory with a triple-double, recording an impressive stat line of 42 points, 12 rebounds, and 10 assists. But it was the intangibles that truly set him apart. His leadership, determination, and unwavering belief in his abilities propelled the Miami Heat to a crucial victory. More importantly, it signaled a shift in the narrative surrounding LeBron James. He had proven that he could deliver on the biggest stage, that he was a player capable of rising to the occasion when it mattered most.

The Redemption Game became a turning point not only for LeBron James but for the Miami Heat as a whole. Buoyed by their superstar's performance, they carried the momentum into the remaining games of the series. They fought tooth and nail, refusing to back down, and ultimately emerged victorious, capturing the NBA Championship.

For LeBron James, the Redemption Game marked a personal triumph. It was a statement to the world that he had overcome adversity, silencing the critics and cementing his legacy as one of the greatest players of all time. It was a redemption not just for himself but for the entire journey he had embarked upon. The decision to join the Miami Heat, the trials and tribulations faced along the way—all of it culminated in this moment of redemption.

Beyond the individual accolades, LeBron James' Redemption Game resonated with fans worldwide. It became an inspiration for those facing their own challenges, a reminder to persevere, and a testament to the power of resilience. The game exemplified the never-give-up spirit that defines sports, reminding us that setbacks can be transformed into stepping stones toward success.

The Redemption Game also had far-reaching implications for the Miami Heat organization. It solidified their status as champions, establishing a winning culture that would define their subsequent seasons. It served as a rallying cry for the team and its fans, a reminder of what could be achieved through hard work, determination, and unwavering belief.

In the years that followed, LeBron James continued to build on his legacy, capturing more championships and earning numerous accolades. But the Redemption Game would forever stand as a pinnacle moment in his career. It represented a transformative period, a time when he faced adversity head-on and emerged stronger, proving that even legends can find redemption in the face of doubt.

THE PERFECT SEASON

The Unyielding Dominance of the Golden State Warriors

"Perfection is not the absence of flaws, but the unwavering pursuit of excellence in spite of them."

- Stephen Curry

The Golden State Warriors entered the 2015-2016 NBA season with a determination burning in their hearts. After falling short in the previous year's NBA Finals, they were on a mission to make a statement and redefine greatness. Led by the dynamic duo of Stephen Curry and Klay Thompson, the Warriors aimed to embark on a quest for the perfect season.

From the very beginning, the Warriors displayed an unyielding dominance. They stormed out of the gates, winning their first 24 games of the season—a new NBA record for the best start in history. Stephen Curry, with his mesmerizing shooting displays and seemingly limitless range, became the talk of the league. His ability to drain three-pointers from unimaginable distances captivated fans and bewildered opponents. Curry's unprecedented shooting skills and the team's suffocating defense propelled the Warriors to victory after victory.

As the season progressed, the challenges grew in intensity. Injuries plagued the team, threatening to derail their pursuit of perfection. But the Warriors refused to succumb to adversity. Their resilience and unwavering focus carried them through the toughest of times. They encountered grueling road trips, battled against teams desperate to end their winning streak, and faced constant scrutiny from the media. Yet, they stood strong, united in their pursuit of greatness.

The Warriors' success was not solely due to the brilliance of Curry and Thompson. It was a collective effort, a symphony of talents working in perfect harmony. Draymond Green's tenacious defense and playmaking abilities, Andre Iguodala's veteran leadership, and the contributions of the supporting cast all played crucial roles in the team's dominance. They embraced their roles and selflessly sacrificed personal glory for the greater good of the team.

Throughout the season, the Warriors captivated fans with their fast-paced, high-scoring style of play. Their "Strength in Numbers" philosophy embodied unselfishness and team-first mentality. They moved the ball with precision, exploiting defensive weaknesses and leaving opponents scrambling to keep up. The combination of Curry's otherworldly shooting,

Thompson's sharpshooting prowess, and the team's unrelenting intensity on both ends of the court made them an unstoppable force.

Despite their remarkable success, the Warriors faced their fair share of adversity. In February, they experienced a humbling loss to the Portland Trail Blazers, ending their record-breaking 54-game home winning streak. It served as a wake-up call, a reminder that perfection is elusive and that even the best teams have their vulnerabilities. The loss, rather than breaking their spirit, fueled their determination to get back on track.

As the regular season drew to a close, the Warriors found themselves on the cusp of history. With a record of 72 wins and 9 losses, they were on the verge of surpassing the 1995-1996 Chicago Bulls' record of 72-10—a feat once thought to be unbreakable. The basketball world held its breath as the Warriors faced the Memphis Grizzlies in their final game of the season. The weight of the moment was palpable, but the Warriors embraced the pressure and emerged victorious, securing their place in basketball history with a record-setting 73rd win.

The perfect season was a testament to the Warriors' unwavering commitment to excellence. It represented their dedication, unity, and relentless pursuit of perfection. They had etched their names in the annals of basketball history, forever remembered as one of the greatest teams to have graced the hardwood.

But beyond the wins and records, the perfect season left an indelible mark on the sport and its fans. It became a symbol of what can be achieved through hard work, resilience, and a shared vision. The Warriors inspired a generation of players and fans alike, reminding them that greatness is not just achieved; it is earned through dedication, unity, and an unwavering pursuit of perfection.

The perfect season was not without its critics, of course. Some argued that the Warriors' success was fueled by their superior shooting and offensive firepower rather than their defensive prowess. However, what set the Warriors apart was their ability to adapt and thrive under pressure. As opposing teams adjusted their strategies to contain Curry, the rest of the team stepped up to fill the void. Klay Thompson's scoring prowess, Draymond Green's playmaking abilities, and the contributions from the bench became instrumental in maintaining the team's dominance. The Warriors' ability to seamlessly adjust and find success in different situations showcased their versatility and basketball IQ.

Moreover, the perfect season served as a platform for Stephen Curry's meteoric rise to superstardom. His electrifying style of play, coupled with his infectious joy for the game, endeared him not only to Warriors fans but to basketball enthusiasts worldwide.

Curry's impact extended beyond his on-court performance. He revolutionized the way the game was played, inspiring a new generation of players to embrace the three-point shot and push the boundaries of what was deemed possible. His influence transcended statistics, sparking a shift in the NBA landscape and forever changing the way the game is perceived. In fact, in the modern day of memes and internet fame, many young fans often made edits of him achieving great feats on the court. One such edit is of him dribbling on the court and losing the ball, and realizing that the court had a weak spot. Everyone was amazed that he knew that he was so good that the problem wasn't his dribbling but the floor. Truly an epic moment in basketball.

THE EUROSTEP MAESTRO

Manu Ginobili and the San Antonio Spurs

"Every step is a canvas, every defender a brushstroke. The Eurostep allows me to paint a masterpiece on the court."

- Manu Ginobili

Manu Ginobili, a basketball virtuoso hailing from Argentina, emerged as a force to be reckoned with in the world of professional basketball. His journey to becoming one of the most respected players in the NBA was a testament to his unwavering determination, unrelenting work ethic, and unique ability to execute the Eurostep—a move that would forever alter the landscape of the game.

Ginobili's early years were marked by his love for basketball. Growing up in Bahia Blanca, Argentina, he displayed a natural talent for the sport. He honed his skills on the courts of his hometown, developing a versatile game that would set him apart from his peers. Ginobili's passion for the game and his relentless drive to improve earned him a scholarship to play college basketball in the United States.

After an impressive collegiate career, Ginobili was selected by the San Antonio Spurs in the 1999 NBA Draft. From the moment he stepped foot on the NBA court, it was clear that Ginobili possessed a unique skill set. His ability to navigate through traffic, evade defenders, and finish at the rim with finesse set him apart from other players. But it was his execution of the Eurostep that truly showcased his mastery of the game.

The Eurostep, a move popularized in European basketball, involves a quick change of direction while driving to the basket. It requires precise footwork, body control, and the ability to deceive defenders. Ginobili took the Eurostep to new heights, elevating it from a mere move to a work of art. With his crafty footwork and impeccable timing, he weaved through defenses, leaving opponents flat-footed and in awe of his evasive elegance.

Ginobili's Eurostep became a signature move that defined his playing style. With each Eurostep, he showcased his creativity, intelligence, and his uncanny ability to exploit defensive weaknesses. He utilized the move in a variety of situations, whether in transition, attacking the rim, or creating scoring opportunities for his teammates. The Eurostep was not just a means to an end for Ginobili; it was an expression of his basketball IQ and his unique understanding of the game.

Opponents struggled to contain Ginobili's Eurostep, as it seemed to defy the laws of physics. His seamless transitions, combined with his ability to finish with either hand, made him a nightmare for defenses. No matter how well-prepared opponents were, they found themselves at a disadvantage when faced with Ginobili's Eurostep. It was a move that left defenders guessing, second-guessing, and ultimately scrambling to recover.

But Ginobili's impact extended beyond his execution of the Eurostep. His competitive spirit, selflessness, and team-first mentality made him a beloved figure both on and off the court. He embraced his role as the sixth man for the San Antonio Spurs, providing a spark off the bench and elevating the play of his teammates. Ginobili's willingness to sacrifice personal accolades for the greater good of the team became a hallmark of his career.

Ginobili's Eurostep not only captivated fans but also influenced a generation of basketball players. As his fame spread, aspiring players sought to replicate his moves, emulate his style, and incorporate the Eurostep into their own games. The move became a staple in playgrounds, gyms, and basketball courts around the world. The Eurostep became synonymous with Ginobili—a testament to his impact on the game.

Throughout his career, Ginobili's Eurostep proved to be an invaluable weapon for the San Antonio Spurs. It played a crucial role in the team's success, helping them secure multiple NBA championships. With Ginobili leading the charge, the Spurs became a powerhouse in the NBA, admired for their precision, teamwork, and strategic play. The Eurostep, in the hands of Ginobili, became a symbol of the Spurs' success.

Beyond the court, Ginobili's influence extended into the hearts of fans. He became a beloved figure, not just for his on-court achievements but also for his humility, sportsmanship, and love for the game. Fans marveled at his passion, intensity, and unwavering dedication to the sport. Ginobili's impact went beyond the statistics; it was his infectious energy and genuine love for the game that endeared him to fans across the globe.

As the years went by, Ginobili's skills and athleticism began to wane, but his basketball IQ and craftiness remained intact. He adapted his game, relying more on experience and knowledge rather than sheer physicality. His Eurostep continued to be effective, serving as a reminder of his brilliance and mastery of the move. Even as younger players entered the league, Ginobili's Eurostep remained a symbol of his greatness and an inspiration to those who followed in his footsteps.

Ginobili's illustrious career came to a close in 2018 when he announced his retirement from professional basketball. The news sent shockwaves through the basketball community, as fans and players alike paid tribute to his legacy. His impact on the game, particularly with his Eurostep, was undeniable. Ginobili left a lasting mark on the sport, forever etching his name among the greatest players to have ever graced the hardwood.

The legacy of Manu Ginobili and his Eurostep continues to reverberate throughout the basketball world. Players still study his footwork, attempting to replicate the finesse and precision he displayed on the court. Coaches analyze his moves, looking for ways to incorporate the Eurostep into their teams' offensive strategies. Fans reminisce about the excitement and anticipation that filled the air every time Ginobili drove to the basket, wondering which version of the Eurostep he would unleash.

But perhaps the greatest testament to Ginobili's Eurostep is the way it transcended individual achievements and became a symbol of artistry in basketball. It showcased the beauty of the game, the elegance of skillful execution, and the thrill of witnessing a player at the height of his craft. The Eurostep, in the hands of Manu Ginobili, became more than just a move; it became a work of art—an expression of creativity, finesse, and basketball genius.

THE SHOT CLOCK SAVIOR

Dirk Nowitzki and the Dallas Mavericks

"In the final seconds, with the shot clock winding down, Dirk Nowitzki's precision and poise would save the day, leaving opponents in disbelief and fans in awe."

- a commentator on Dirk Nowitzki

In the world of basketball, there are moments that define a player's career and shape the destiny of a team. Dirk Nowitzki, a towering figure known for his remarkable shooting touch and unwavering determination, became synonymous with clutch performances throughout his illustrious career. Dirk Nowitzki and his role as the Shot Clock Savior for the Dallas Mavericks made a miracle out of his career and inspired many people with the way that he played.

From his early days in Germany to his arrival in the NBA, Nowitzki showcased a unique blend of size, skill, and versatility that set him apart from his peers. Standing at 7 feet tall, with a silky-smooth shooting stroke, he became a force to be reckoned with on the court. However, it was his ability to rise to the occasion when time was running out that would forever cement his legacy as the Shot Clock Savior.

Nowitzki's clutch performances were not merely a result of luck or happenstance; they were a product of his relentless work ethic and unwavering focus. He spent countless hours refining his shooting mechanics, honing his footwork, and studying opponents' defensive schemes. This dedication paid dividends when the clock was ticking down, as Nowitzki seemed to possess an otherworldly ability to create space and deliver the ball through the net with pinpoint accuracy.

Opponents quickly learned to fear Nowitzki in the waning seconds of a game. As the shot clock dwindled and the pressure mounted, he remained composed, undeterred by the intensity of the moment. With his trademark fadeaway jumper, Nowitzki elevated above defenders, releasing the ball with a high arc that seemed to defy gravity. Time and time again, he delivered in the clutch, sinking shots that were nothing short of miraculous.

The Shot Clock Savior moniker was not just a testament to Nowitzki's ability to score in critical moments; it also spoke to his leadership and composure under pressure. He embraced the responsibility of carrying his team's hopes on his shoulders, displaying a calm demeanor and instilling confidence in his teammates. Nowitzki's unflappable nature in the face of adversity inspired those around him, fostering a culture of resilience and determination within the Dallas Mavericks.

One of Nowitzki's most iconic moments as the Shot Clock Savior came during the 2011 NBA Finals. Facing off against the star-studded Miami Heat, the Mavericks found themselves in a grueling battle for the championship. In Game 2, with the score tied and the shot clock winding down, Nowitzki received the ball at the top of the key. As the seconds ticked away, he unleashed a step-back jumper over the outstretched arms of LeBron James, sinking the shot and securing a crucial victory for his team. This clutch performance set the tone for the rest of the series as Nowitzki led the Mavericks to an improbable championship triumph.

But the Shot Clock Savior's heroics extended beyond individual game-winning shots. Nowitzki's ability to consistently deliver in clutch situations brought an intangible element to the Mavericks' offense. His mere presence on the court forced opponents to double-team him, creating opportunities for his teammates to score. Nowitzki's basketball IQ and unselfishness allowed him to make the right play, whether it was sinking a fadeaway jumper or dishing the ball to an open teammate. He understood the gravity of the moment and made the necessary sacrifices to ensure his team's success.

Nowitzki's impact extended beyond the basketball court. His humble and gracious demeanor off the court endeared him to fans and earned the respect of his peers. Nowitzki's dedication to the game and his unwavering commitment to excellence made him a beloved figure, not just in Dallas but across the basketball world.

The Shot Clock Savior's influence was not limited to his playing career. Nowitzki's clutch performances and his ability to rise to the occasion in pressure-packed moments inspired a generation of young players. Aspiring basketball stars looked up to him as a role model, studying his footwork, shooting technique, and mental fortitude. They sought to emulate his composure and learn from his dedication to the craft. Nowitzki's impact on the game extended far beyond the statistics; it was his ability to inspire and motivate that truly set him apart.

As the years went by, Nowitzki's role on the court evolved. His once lightning-quick step and explosive athleticism began to fade, but his basketball IQ and shooting touch remained as lethal as ever. Despite the physical challenges that come with age, Nowitzki continued to be a respected leader on the Mavericks, guiding his team with his experience and knowledge. He embraced his role as a mentor to younger players, imparting wisdom and instilling a sense of purpose in the next generation.

In 2019, Nowitzki announced his retirement, bidding farewell to a career that had spanned over two decades. The basketball world came together to celebrate his remarkable journey and pay tribute to the legacy he left behind. Nowitzki's impact on the Dallas Mavericks and the game of basketball as a whole was immeasurable. He had etched his name among the greatest players to have ever played the game, leaving a lasting impression as the Shot Clock Savior.

Probably the biggest accolade of Nowitzki's career was the big up he got from Kobe Bryant, who said in a long speech that "Dirk Nowitzki was a basketball genius, a maestro of the game whose performance on the court was nothing short of extraordinary. His ability to rise to the occasion in clutch moments and deliver game-winning shots left us in awe. Dirk had a unique combination of size, skill, and basketball IQ that made him virtually unstoppable. He could shoot from anywhere on the court, his fadeaway jumper was a thing of beauty, and his footwork was unparalleled. But what truly set Dirk apart was his mental toughness and composure under pressure. He thrived in the biggest moments, taking on the responsibility of carrying his team to victory. His unwavering determination and relentless work ethic were an inspiration to us all. Dirk's impact on the game extended far beyond his individual achievements. He revolutionized the power forward position, showcasing the importance of shooting and versatility in today's NBA. His influence will be felt for generations to come. Dirk Nowitzki was not just a great player; he was a legend, a true ambassador of the game, and a role model for aspiring basketball players around the world."

THE CINDERELLA STORY

The Villanova Wildcats and the 1985 NCAA Championship

"Villanova's remarkable Cinderella story in 1985 is a shining example of the resilience and determination that defines sports. It reminds us that in the face of adversity, true champions rise. The Wildcats' triumph is a testament to the indomitable human spirit."

- Jay Wright

In the world of sports, few moments captivate our imagination and embody the essence of the underdog quite like a Cinderella story. Such was the case in the 1985 NCAA Championship when the Villanova Wildcats, a team not favored to win, defied the odds and etched their names into college basketball history. This chapter delves into the remarkable journey of the Villanova Wildcats and their incredible run to become champions.

The 1985 NCAA Tournament was full of excitement and anticipation as the best college basketball teams from around the country gathered to compete for the coveted national title. The

Wildcats, led by their head coach, Rollie Massimino, entered the tournament as the eighth seed in the Southeast Region. While their regular season had shown promise, few expected them to make a deep run in the tournament, let alone reach the championship game.

The road to the championship was anything but easy for Villanova. They faced formidable opponents at every turn, but their resilience, teamwork, and unwavering belief propelled them forward. In the first round, they squared off against the heavily favored Dayton Flyers, and against all odds, the Wildcats emerged victorious, shocking the college basketball world. This early upset set the stage for what would become a Cinderella story of epic proportions.

As the tournament progressed, Villanova continued to defy expectations. In the Sweet Sixteen, they faced the number one seed, the Michigan Wolverines, led by their star forward, Roy Tarpley. Despite being the clear underdogs, the Wildcats displayed exceptional poise and determination, executing their game plan flawlessly. Their precision shooting, unyielding defense, and the leadership of their senior guard, Harold Jensen, propelled them to a stunning victory, advancing them to the Elite Eight.

In the Elite Eight, the Wildcats faced yet another formidable opponent in the North Carolina Tar Heels, led by their head coach, Dean Smith. The game was a back-and-forth battle, with both teams showcasing their skills and competitive spirit. The Wildcats' tenacious defense and clutch shooting allowed them to secure a hard-fought victory, propelling them to the Final Four for the first time since 1971.

The Final Four stage was set, and Villanova found themselves facing the top-ranked team in the country, the Memphis State Tigers, coached by the legendary Larry Finch. The Tigers boasted an impressive roster led by their star center, Keith Lee. However, the Wildcats were undeterred by the Tigers' reputation and played with unwavering confidence. In a thrilling and closely contested matchup, Villanova emerged victorious, securing their place in the championship game.

The stage was set for the championship showdown between the Villanova Wildcats and the Georgetown Hoyas, led by their dominant center, Patrick Ewing. The Hoyas were the overwhelming favorites, a powerhouse team that had been a dominant force throughout the season. But the Wildcats had a game plan that would go down in history as one of the most brilliant and executed to perfection.

In the championship game, played on April 1, 1985, at Rupp Arena in Lexington, Kentucky, the Wildcats took to the court with an unwavering belief in their abilities. They executed their offense with precision, shooting an astonishing 79% from the field, a record that still stands in NCAA championship game history. The Wildcats' ball movement, patience, and discipline against Georgetown's vaunted defense allowed them to control the tempo and keep the game within their reach.

As the game entered its final minutes, Villanova found themselves in a nail-biting battle. With the score tied at 52-52, the Wildcats seized the moment. Harold Jensen, the unsung hero of the tournament, stepped up with a clutch three-pointer, giving Villanova a three-point lead with just over two minutes remaining. The shot ignited a frenzy among the Wildcats' fans, who could feel history in the making.

The final moments of the game were a testament to the Wildcats' resilience and composure. They held their ground against a fierce Georgetown comeback attempt, making crucial free throws and securing crucial defensive stops. As the clock ticked down, the Villanova faithful held their breath, knowing that their team was on the verge of achieving the unthinkable.

When the final buzzer sounded, it marked the end of an incredible journey for the Villanova Wildcats. They had done it. Against all odds, they had toppled the mighty Georgetown Hoyas with a final score of 66-64. The celebration that followed was a testament to the sheer joy and disbelief that engulfed the players, coaches, and fans alike. The Cinderella story had reached its magical conclusion.

The Villanova Wildcats' triumph in the 1985 NCAA Championship left an indelible mark on college basketball history. Their incredible run as an eighth seed to claim the title demonstrated the power of belief, teamwork, and the ability to rise to the occasion when it matters most. It served as a reminder that in sports, anything is possible, and that the underdog can indeed conquer the giants.

The impact of Villanova's victory went beyond the court. It inspired a generation of basketball players and fans, showing them that dreams can become a reality with hard work, dedication, and a never-give-up attitude. The Wildcats' remarkable accomplishment brought a sense of hope and inspiration to the basketball community, forever cementing their place as one of the greatest Cinderella stories in sports history.

In the years following their historic triumph, the Villanova Wildcats continued to build on their success. They became a perennial contender in college basketball, making regular appearances in the NCAA Tournament and consistently showcasing their trademark grit and determination. The 1985 championship team served as a foundation upon which the program flourished, etching their name among the elite in college basketball.

Beyond the confines of Villanova's campus, the impact of their Cinderella story resonated with basketball enthusiasts worldwide. It became a symbol of hope for underdogs everywhere, a shining example that with belief, perseverance, and the right combination of talent and strategy, anything is achievable. The Villanova Wildcats showed the world that dreams can come true, even when the odds are stacked against you.

THE UPSET OF THE CENTURY

The 16th-seeded UMBC Retrievers
defeating the 1st-seeded Virginia Cavaliers
in the 2018 NCAA Tournament

*"Believe in yourself and all that you are. Know that there is
something inside you that is greater than any obstacle."*

- Christian D. Larson

I n the annals of college basketball history, there are few
moments that can rival the magnitude and impact of an
unforgettable upset. Such was the case when an extraordinary
event unfolded during the NCAA Tournament, forever etching
itself into the hearts and minds of basketball fans around the
world.

The stage was set for the ultimate David versus Goliath
showdown. The Virginia Cavaliers, a powerhouse program with
a stellar regular season record, entered the tournament as the
overwhelming favorites. They were the embodiment of
dominance, led by their star player, a formidable lineup, and the
steady hand of their esteemed coach, Tony Bennett. The

Cavaliers were expected to cruise past their first-round opponents, the UMBC Retrievers, a relatively unknown team from a smaller conference.

The Retrievers, however, had a different plan in mind. Led by their fearless coach, Ryan Odom, and a roster of talented players, they embraced their underdog status and stepped onto the court with unwavering belief. They were ready to challenge the narrative and prove that anything is possible in the game of basketball.

As the game tipped off, the Retrievers showcased their grit and determination from the opening whistle. They played with relentless energy, executing their game plan flawlessly. The Cavaliers, caught off guard by the intensity and tenacity of their opponents, found themselves on the back foot. The Retrievers' suffocating defense, combined with their sharp shooting and precise execution on offense, allowed them to build a surprising lead.

As the game progressed, the Retrievers' confidence grew. Every shot they took seemed to find its mark, and their defense continued to stifle the Cavaliers' offensive efforts. The atmosphere inside the arena was electric as the underdog team from UMBC captivated the audience with their remarkable performance. Fans and viewers around the world watched in awe as a historic upset slowly unfolded before their eyes.

As the final seconds ticked away, it became apparent that the impossible was indeed happening. The UMBC Retrievers had done the unthinkable. They had toppled the mighty Virginia Cavaliers, marking the first time in NCAA Tournament history that a 16th-seeded team had defeated a top-seeded team. The Retrievers' 74-54 victory sent shockwaves through the basketball world, leaving fans, analysts, and even the players themselves in disbelief.

The aftermath of this monumental upset was profound. The Retrievers became overnight sensations, capturing the hearts of basketball enthusiasts everywhere. Their journey inspired countless underdog teams and reminded everyone that no matter the odds, with dedication, belief, and unwavering determination, greatness can be achieved.

For the Cavaliers, the loss was a bitter pill to swallow. Their dreams of a championship had been shattered in an unprecedented fashion. However, their response to the defeat was a testament to their character and the resilience instilled in them by their coach. They used the setback as fuel for future success, returning to the tournament the following year with a renewed sense of purpose and determination.

The UMBC Retrievers' victory over the Virginia Cavaliers will forever be etched in the history books as one of the most remarkable upsets in sports. It serves as a reminder that in the game of basketball and in life, anything is possible. The

Retrievers' triumph exemplifies the power of belief, teamwork, and the ability to rise to the occasion when the world is watching.

The impact of this monumental upset extended far beyond the basketball court. The Retrievers' victory captured the imagination of sports fans worldwide, rekindling the belief that dreams can come true, no matter the circumstances. It became a symbol of hope and inspiration for underdog teams in all sports, reminding them that they should never underestimate their potential and always strive to defy expectations.

The UMBC Retrievers became overnight sensations, their names etched in the hearts of basketball fans everywhere. The players and coaching staff were celebrated as heroes, their journey immortalized in the annals of sports history. They became a beacon of hope for all those who had ever been counted out, showcasing the power of resilience and determination in the face of adversity.

For the Virginia Cavaliers, the loss served as a humbling reminder of the unpredictable nature of sports. It challenged them to reassess their approach and instilled a deeper hunger for success. The defeat fueled their determination to come back stronger, using it as motivation to push themselves further in their pursuit of greatness.

In the years following the historic upset, the UMBC

Retrievers' achievement continued to reverberate through the basketball landscape. Their story inspired countless underdog teams and served as a constant reminder of the power of belief and the potential for greatness in every game.

The impact of the upset extended beyond the realm of sports. It transcended boundaries and touched the hearts of individuals from all walks of life. It became a source of inspiration, reminding people that they should never be limited by others' expectations and should always strive to challenge the status quo.

The UMBC Retrievers' victory also sparked discussions and debates about the nature of sports, the unpredictability of competition, and the significance of the underdog narrative. It highlighted the beauty of sports, where anything can happen on any given day and where the human spirit can triumph against all odds.

The event serves as a powerful reminder that sports have the ability to captivate, inspire, and bring people together. It showcases the transformative power of a single moment, where a team's belief in themselves can shatter long-standing perceptions and rewrite history books.

CONCLUSION

Who would have ever thought that it's possible to play a professional basketball game while battling with flu? Or that one person could have the talent and stamina to basically carry an entire team through the Olympics, giving their team a miraculous win? In fact, what are the odds that a fight would physically break out on the professional court and that would change the precautions taken during matches forevermore? If we're being honest, these scenarios are a basketball mirror version(just think Black Mirror except with basketball) of our lives.

I think most mothers can attest to the fact that they have had to finish what seemed like Herculean tasks of managing the house and getting everything done while suffering from a splitting headache, little sleep, and flu. They would definitely understand how much determination Jordan needed to play while sick and get the job done. The enthusiastic intern can probably relate to what it's like to basically be doing the job of five people while also attending to endless calls for coffee refills, which seems a lot like how Kobe Byrant had to carry the entire team on his back during the Olympics. And I think almost anyone can relate to how underlying tension with another person or group spilled over and caused an unnecessary conflict. It might even just be being able to relate to people's perception of you changing after making a mistake. At the end of the day, basketball resonates with us so much because we see a part of ourselves in the players, the events, and the teams.

In essence, we are not so far removed or far off from the basketball stars and events that we so admire and adore, which means that someday, we can also take our shot and maybe end up in someone's book of greats.

As we reach the end of this journey through basketball's most amazing events, we are reminded of the profound impact this sport has had on our lives. From buzzer-beaters to dominant dynasties, rivalries to individual brilliance, each chapter has revealed the power and beauty of basketball in its own unique way. Through these stories, we have witnessed the heights of human achievement, the depths of resilience, and the unbreakable spirit that fuels the game we love.

This book has served as a tribute to the rich history of basketball and the extraordinary individuals who have shaped it.

From the pioneers who paved the way for future generations to the modern-day legends who continue to push the boundaries of what is possible, their stories have left an indelible mark on the sport and inspired countless fans around the world.

The significance of these amazing basketball events extends far beyond the confines of the court. They have become part of our cultural fabric, symbols of triumph, determination, and the unyielding pursuit of greatness. They have given us moments of joy, heartbreak, and everything in between. But most importantly, they have brought people together, creating a sense of community and shared experiences that transcend boundaries.

Through these stories, we have learned valuable lessons about perseverance, teamwork, and the power of belief. We have seen how the human spirit can overcome adversity, how a single moment can change the course of a game, and how the collective efforts of a team can lead to greatness. These lessons resonate within the realm of basketball and our lives, reminding us of the power we hold within ourselves to achieve our goals and overcome obstacles.

As we reflect on the significance of these amazing events, we are reminded that basketball is more than just a game. It is a vehicle for inspiration, a catalyst for change, and a source of joy and unity. It can transcend cultural, social, and economic barriers, bringing people from all walks of life together in a shared passion. It teaches us the values of discipline, sportsmanship, and the pursuit of excellence.

To the readers who have embarked on this journey, we hope that you have gained a deeper appreciation for the beauty and significance of basketball's most amazing events. We hope that these stories have brought back cherished memories, sparked conversations, and reignited your passion for the game. But above all, we hope they have inspired you to believe in the power of your dreams and the potential for greatness within you.

At the end of this book, we encourage you to carry the spirit of these amazing events with you in your own lives. Let the lessons learned from the likes of Michael Jordan, Magic Johnson, and countless others serve as a constant reminder of what is possible when we dedicate ourselves to our craft and embrace the challenges that come our way. Let their stories inspire you to push beyond your limits, pursue your passions with unwavering determination, and always believe in the power of teamwork and camaraderie.

In a world that is often divided, sports have a unique ability to bring people together, to bridge gaps, and to foster understanding. Basketball, with its amazing events and storied history, has played a significant role in uniting people from all walks of life. As fans, we have witnessed the magic that unfolds on the court, and it is our responsibility to carry that spirit of unity and sportsmanship beyond the game.

So, as we bid farewell to the amazing events that have shaped the world of basketball, let us remember their impact on our lives. Let us celebrate the moments of triumph, the displays of skill, and the stories of resilience. And let us continue to embrace the spirit of basketball, both on and off the court, as we strive to create a better world fueled by passion, perseverance, and the pursuit of greatness.

In closing, we hope that this book has taken you on a captivating journey through the annals of basketball history. We have explored the iconic moments, the legendary players, and the unforgettable narratives that have made basketball the global phenomenon it is today. These amazing events have left an indelible mark on the sport, etching themselves into the collective memory of fans across the world.

But beyond the entertainment value and the thrill of the game, the significance of these events lies in the lessons they impart. They teach us about the power of determination, the value of teamwork, and the resilience of the human spirit. They inspire us to dream big, to pursue our goals with unwavering passion, and to never give up in the face of adversity.

Moreover, the stories of these amazing events are a testament to the unifying power of sports. They transcend cultural boundaries, language barriers, and societal divisions, bringing people together under the common language of basketball. In a world often marked by differences, these events remind us of our shared humanity, our shared love for the game, and our capacity to come together as a global community.

As you close this book, we hope that you carry the spirit of these amazing events with you. Let their stories fuel your own aspirations, ignite your competitive fire, and inspire you to make a positive impact in your own life and the lives of others. Let them remind you that greatness can be achieved through hard work, perseverance, and a relentless pursuit of excellence.

And finally, we encourage you to share these stories with others. Pass on the knowledge, the inspiration, and the joy that basketball's amazing events have brought you. Engage in discussions, debates, and celebrations of the sport. Let the magic of these moments continue to captivate future generations and keep the spirit of basketball alive.

In the end, basketball is more than just a game. It is a celebration of human potential, a testament to the power of dreams, and a symbol of unity and camaraderie. The amazing events that have unfolded within the realm of basketball have left an everlasting legacy, shaping the sport and inspiring generations of players and fans alike.

Let's carry the memories of these amazing events in our hearts and minds. Let us honor the legends who have graced the court, the teams that have captivated us, and the moments that have left us breathless. And let us continue to write new chapters in the story of basketball, creating our own amazing events and contributing to the ever-evolving tapestry of this beautiful sport.

Thank you for joining us on this journey through basketball's most amazing events. May the lessons learned, the memories cherished, and the passion ignited stay with you as you continue to follow the game you love. Remember, the story of basketball is far from over. There are still countless amazing events waiting to be written, and you have the power to be a part of them. Embrace the game, embrace the moments, and embrace the incredible journey that is basketball.

About Us

All-Star Reads: Where Sports + Imagination Collide

All-Star Reads is a premier publishing company passionate about fostering a love for reading while celebrating the excitement of sportsmanship!

With a blend of informative content and imaginative storytelling, we're committed to creating books that encourage important life values such as teamwork, perseverance, and determination.

Join us in this adventure where each page is a slam dunk of discovery and every chapter unfolds a new victory.

Thanks for reading,

Review Club

FREE BESTSELLING BOOKS

☆ ☆ ☆ ☆ ☆ ☆ ☆

1   Leave a quick review of the book

USA	CANADA	UK	AUSTRALIA

2   Download each week's FREE Kindle Book

DOWNLOAD

3   That's It. Thank you!

www.kindlepromos.com/club

Made in United States
Troutdale, OR
05/01/2024

19556382R00072